getting CRAFTY

NATURE PROJECTS

written by
DANA MEACHEN RAU

45th Parallel Press

Published in the United States of America by Cherry Lake Publishing Group
Ann Arbor, Michigan
www.cherrylakepublishing.com

Reading Adviser: Beth Walker Gambro, MS, Ed., Reading Consultant, Yorkville, IL
Illustrator: Ashley Dugan
Book Designer: Felicia Macheske

Photo Credits: © jessicahyde/Shutterstock, 4; © Jonathan Caillot/Shutterstock, 5; © Pheobus/Shutterstock, 6; © Auhustsinovich/Shutterstock, 7

45th Parallel Press is an imprint of Cherry Lake Publishing Group.

Library of Congress Cataloging-in-Publication Data

Names: Rau, Dana Meachen, 1971- author. | Dugan, Ashley, illustrator.
Title: Nature projects / written by Dana Meachen Rau ; illustrated by Ashley Dugan.
Description: Ann Arbor, Michigan : Cherry Lake Publishing, [2023] | Series: Getting crafty | Includes bibliographical references and index. | Audience: Grades 4-6 | Summary: "Take a hike and explore your creative side! Discover new skills and get crafty with nature. Learn how to make grapevine wreaths, shell wind chimes and more! Book includes an introduction to exploring nature and the history of creating art from nature. It also includes several projects with easy-to-follow step-by-step instructions and illustrations. Book is developed to aid struggling and reluctant readers with engaging content, carefully chosen vocabulary, and simple sentences. Includes table of contents, glossary, index, sidebars, and author biographies"—Provided by publisher.
Identifiers: LCCN 2022041829 | ISBN 9781668919590 (hardcover) | ISBN 9781668920619 (paperback) | ISBN 9781668921944 (ebook) | ISBN 9781668923276 (pdf)
Subjects: LCSH: Nature craft—Juvenile literature.
Classification: LCC TT160 .R3823 2023 | DDC 745.5—dc23/eng/20220902
LC record available at https://lccn.loc.gov/2022041829

Cherry Lake Publishing Group would like to acknowledge the work of the Partnership for 21st Century Learning, a Network of Battelle for Kids. Please visit *http://www.battelleforkids.org/networks/p21* for more information.

Printed in the United States of America
Corporate Graphics

TABLE of CONTENTS

TAKE A HIKE! 4

NATURAL RESOURCES 6

OUTDOOR SUPPLIES 8

INDOOR SUPPLIES 10

GRAPEVINE WREATH 12

PINE SACHET 14

FOSSIL STEPPING-STONE 16

SHELL WIND CHIMES 18

HAMMERED LEAF PRINTS 20

PRESSED FLOWER PICTURE 22

SAND CANDLES 25

CRITTER-FRIENDLY CORNER 28

INSPIRATION EVERY DAY 29

Glossary 30

For More Information 31

Index 32

TAKE A HIKE!

Explore the natural world around you. Take a stroll in the woods. Wander through a meadow. Walk along the shore. You might live near mountains. Or a desert. Or along a river. There is so much to see in nature.

Look at how a tree displays its leaves. Look at how a spider builds its web. See how wind makes grass sway. Check out the shape of a flock of birds in flight. Nature is a marvel.

Nature is also full of color. The setting sun paints the sky. It makes it orange, red, and purple. Plants are often green. But they may bloom with a rainbow of flowers. They may grow a rainbow of fruit. Find new **textures**. Check tree bark, rocks, or the sharp points of a cactus!

Nature has always been an inspiration for artists. So take a hike outdoors. Gather some craft ideas! Nature can also provide lots of craft materials. Transform bits of the beauty you find outside. Turn them into a piece of art!

WHAT IS NATURE LIKE WHERE YOU LIVE?

Biomes are areas defined by the types of plants, animals, and weather found there. Here are some of the world's biomes:

- Forests
- Savanna
- Tundra
- Grasslands
- Deserts
- Aquatic

NATURAL RESOURCES

People used to use the land's gifts to make useful objects. They made beautiful objects. This was before craft stores. It was before art supply stores. The first artists used **minerals** to paint pictures on cave walls. They used clay to make bowls. They used grasses to weave baskets. They discovered metal in the ground. They melted and molded it to make tools and jewelry.

Children played with dolls made from cornhusks. People wrote with the sharp tips of long feathers dipped in ink. Shells were used to decorate clothing.

Fabric has been, and still is, made from all sorts of natural materials. Wool comes from sheep. Silk comes from the cocoons of silkworms. Cotton fabric comes from the cotton plant. Linen is made from a plant called flax. Trees are used to make paper. Sand is used to make glass.

Natural materials are all around you. How will you use them to make something beautiful?

OUTDOOR SUPPLIES

Think of the outdoors as one huge craft store. Grab a basket and start "shopping." The best part is everything is free! Some useful outdoor supplies include:

Leaves and pine needles

Flowers

Pinecones, acorns, and other seeds

Berries

Grapevines

Rocks, pebbles, and sand

Remember to be a responsible collector. **That is important!**
A responsible collector remembers these tips:

- Look for dead or fallen items first. Pine needles, dried leaves, empty shells, and rocks are not alive. You are not disturbing nature too much if you remove small amounts of these materials.

- Check with an adult before picking anything from a living plant. You don't want to pick something poisonous! Also, be sure you are not picking a plant that may be **endangered**.

- Never take materials from someone else's yard without asking.

- Watch out for animals. Never disturb a wasp's nest. Don't take eggs out of a bird's nest. Never cover the hole of an underground **burrow**.

- Try not to disturb nature. Try to leave an area just as you found it.

INDOOR SUPPLIES

You will need natural materials. You will also need some craft supplies. You will need scissors, a ruler, white glue, double-stick tape, and rope or string. You will also need white paper, cardboard, cardstock paper, and watercolor paper.

Get out a toolbox and garden supplies for some of the projects in this book! You will need a hammer, an electric drill (always ask an adult to help), paddle wire, pruning sheers, gardening gloves, plastic buckets, pots, concrete, and old candles.

PAINTING TIPS

Be sure to protect your work area with newspaper. Use a paper plate as a **palette**. Use it to hold and mix your paint. Keep a container of water handy. Use it to clean your brush between colors. Use a paper towel to **blot** water and paint off your brush.

SEWING TIPS

Thread a needle by holding it steady at the pointy end. Poke the thread through the eye of the needle. Pull it through. Pull until the ends of the thread meet. Tie them in a knot.

Make a blanket stitch by poking the needle into the fabric from the front. Do this about 0.25 inches (0.6 centimeters) from the edge. Pull it through. Then poke it into the front near the edge again.

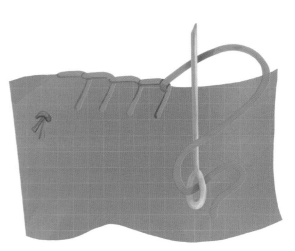

This time, make sure the needle goes through the loop made by the thread. Repeat this stitch all around your piece.

Secure the end of the stitch by poking the needle in and out again very close together. Don't pull it all the way through. Instead, make sure the needle goes through the loop made by the thread. Then pull it tight. Repeat to make a double knot.

GRAPEVINE WREATH

Grapevines often grow delicious fruit. But some wild grapevines grow on young trees. They can make the trees bend under the heavy weight. Help the tree! Pull off some of the vines. Make a wreath you can display in every season!

MATERIALS

- Gardening gloves
- Pruning shears
- 4 or 5 lengths of grapevine, each about 6 to 12 feet (1.8 to 3.7 meters) long
- Natural decorations, such as dried flowers, pinecones, sprigs of berries, or pieces of evergreen
- Wire cutters
- Paddle wire

STEPS

1. Put on your gloves. Ask an adult to help you find a good crop of grapevines. Use the shears. Snip the vines near their base. Pull them out of the branches of the tree. Be careful! It may feel like a tug-of-war!

2. Separate out the best vines. They shouldn't be too thick. You need them to be flexible. Remove the leaves as you untangle the vines. Cut off any branches. Leave the curly **tendrils**. They will add natural details to your wreath. Keep the vines as long as possible.

3. Hold the end of the longest vine in one hand. Loop the vine into a circle shape. This circle can be as large or small as you wish. An 18- to 20-inch (46 to 51 cm) circle is a good size.

4. Next, weave the other end of the vine in and out around the circle. Keep weaving until you reach the end of the vine. Tuck the end into the wreath.

5. Tuck the end of the next vine into the wreath. Weave in and out around the circle as in step 4. Keep adding vines. Weave them around until the wreath is as thick as you want. Let your wreath sit for a few days. It will dry out.

6. Decorate it with natural items. Tuck them into the spaces between the vines. Cut a 12-inch (30 cm) length of paddle wire. Thread it through the top of the wreath. Twist the ends together. Make a loop for hanging.

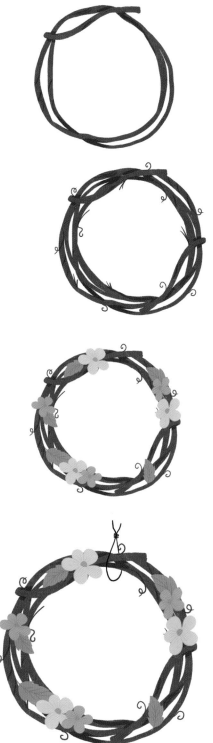

PINE SACHET

Pine needles smell great. Bring this natural perfume indoors with a **sachet**.

MATERIALS

- Newspaper
- 5-inch by 10-inch (12.7 by 25 cm) piece of unbleached muslin
- Green acrylic paint
- Paintbrush, paper plate to use as palette, paper towel, and container of water (see painting tips on page 10)
- Pinecone
- Dried pine needles
- Straight pins
- Brown thread
- Sewing needle
- Scissors

STEPS

1. Cover your workspace with newspaper. Lay your muslin out flat. Squeeze a little paint onto your palette. Lightly paint the side of the pinecone. Press it onto the fabric like a stamp. Keep stamping to create a design on your fabric. Reapply paint to your pinecone as needed. Let the fabric dry.

2. Gather dried pine needles. Get them from the ground outdoors. For one sachet, you will need about 2 cups (473 milliliters) of needles.

3. Fold in the long edges of the muslin about 0.5 inches (1.3 cm). Do this on the back side of the fabric. Then fold the whole thing in half. Pin the folded edges closed on each side. Make a pocket shape with an opening at the top.

4. Start at the open end about 0.5 inches (1.3 cm) down. Sew a blanket stitch around the edges to hold them closed. (See sewing tips on page 11.) Repeat across the folded bottom. Keep going up the other side. Do you still have thread on the needle at the end? You can leave it there for now. Remove the pins as you sew.

5. Fill the pocket from the top with pine needles. Fill until it is full and firm.

6. Fold in the top edges of fabric about 0.5 inches (1.3 cm). Pin the sachet closed. Blanket stitch across the top. This will hold all the pine needles in.

7. Cut any hanging threads.

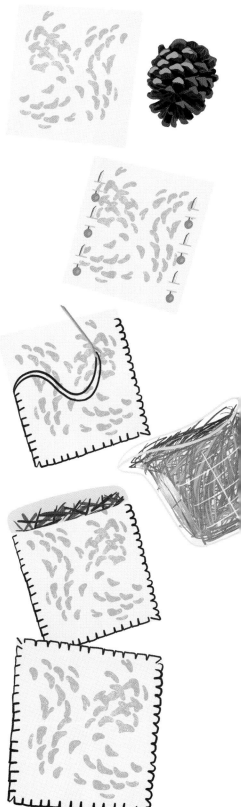

FOSSIL STEPPING-STONE

Walk your way through a garden with a homemade stepping-stone! Add leaf details. It will look like you've unearthed a fossil!

MATERIALS

- Fresh leaves
- 8-inch (20-cm) plastic plant saucer
- Petroleum jelly
- Newspaper
- Plastic gloves
- Face mask
- Safety glasses

- 4 pounds (1.8 kilograms) of concrete (You can find this at home improvement stores or some craft stores.)
- Old bucket
- Water
- Wooden paint stirrer

STEPS

1. Collect some fresh leaves. Make sure the veins on the back of the leaves really stand out. Rub the saucer with petroleum jelly. This will keep the concrete from sticking in your mold.

SAFETY TIPS!

Concrete can be harmful if you breathe in the powder. It can be harmful if you touch it with bare skin. Ask an adult to help you with this project. Wear safety gear. Wear plastic gloves, a face mask, and safety glasses. Clean up the bucket and stirrer outdoors. Or use ones that you can throw away. Wash your hands with warm, soapy water when you're done.

2. Cover your work surface with newspaper. Put on your gloves, mask, and safety glasses.

3. Put the concrete powder into the bucket. Add about 1 cup (237 ml) of water. Mix it with the paint stirrer. Keep adding a little bit more water at a time. Mix after each addition. Do this until you don't see any more powder. The mixture should feel like soft ice cream.

4. Pour the concrete into the plastic saucer. Use the stirrer to level off the top. Make it as flat as possible.

5. Place the leaves, back side down, onto the concrete. Be gentle! Flatten them as best you can. If some of the edges curl up, weigh those spots down with small stones. Don't let the stones touch the concrete. They'll stick!

6. Let your stepping-stone sit in a place where it won't be bothered. Let it sit for about 24 to 48 hours.

7. Peel off the leaves from the stone. Then take the stone out of the mold. Wait a few more days before you put it in your garden or yard.

SHELL WIND CHIMES

Are you a beachcomber? Do you like to collect shells? You can use your finds to make wind chimes. Ask an adult for help with this project. You will be drilling holes. Use shells that are not too thick.

MATERIALS

- About 15 to 20 shells
- Masking tape
- Scrap wood
- Electric drill with narrow drill bit
- Thin rope
- 7-inch (18-cm) metal ring
- Scissors
- Invisible thread

STEPS

1. Collect shells from the beach. Rinse off any extra sand. Put a piece of tape on each shell where you plan to drill. (The tape will keep the shell from cracking.) Place the shells onto a piece of scrap wood. Ask an adult to help drill a hole in each shell. Set the shells aside.

2. Tie the end of the rope onto the ring. Use a tight knot. Then wind the rope tightly around the ring. When you've reached the spot where you started, tie a knot. Snip the ends.

3. Thread a piece of invisible thread through the hole in one of the shells. Tie a knot. Tie the other end to the edge of the ring. You want the shell to hang down about 2 to 4 inches (5 to 10 cm).

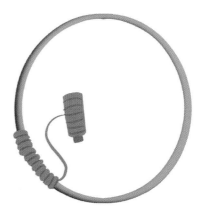

4. Repeat with the rest of the shells. Space them evenly around the ring. Vary their lengths a little bit. Make sure they are close enough to touch each other when the wind blows. Lay your project on a flat surface as you work. This keeps the threads from tangling.

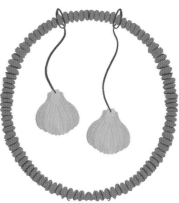

5. To hang your chimes, cut 4 lengths of rope to about 24 inches (61 cm) each. Fold one of the pieces in half. Tuck the looped end under the edge of the ring. Then thread the long ends through the loop. Pull them tight. Repeat with the other pieces of rope evenly spaced around the ring.

6. Gather the loose ends of the ropes into the middle of the ring. Tie them in a knot. Then tie another knot about 2 inches (5 cm) above the first one. This makes a loop for hanging. Trim off the loose ends.

HAMMERED LEAF PRINTS

Send some of the beauty outside your window to friends or family with these notecards. Look for leaves with interesting colors. The leaves have to be fresh. Don't use dry leaves. They won't have enough natural "ink" for this project. (Even if they are colorful!)

MATERIALS

- Fresh leaves
- Watercolor paper
- Old wooden board
- Paper towels
- Hammer (a very small head is best)
- Scissors
- Colored cardstock paper
- White glue or double-stick tape
- White cardstock paper

STEPS

1. Collect interesting leaves.
2. Place the watercolor paper on your board. Then place a leaf facedown onto the paper. Place two pieces of paper towel over the leaf.

3. Hammer the leaf in a few spots. This will help you find its edges. Be careful not to hit your fingers. Keep hammering back and forth. Hammer up and down. Makie sure you hit every part of the leaf. You will be able to see some of the leaf's juices on the paper towel. Take your time. This will take a few minutes. The longer you hammer, the clearer your print will be.

4. Pull back the paper towel. Be careful. See your leaf print. If some bits of the leaf are stuck to the paper, wait for it to dry. Use your fingernail to pull them off.

5. Cut the watercolor paper into a square or rectangle shape around your leaf print. Then choose a color of cardstock paper that goes well with your print. Cut a square or rectangle out of this cardstock. It should be a little bigger than your print. Glue or tape the print onto the colored paper.

6. Fold a piece of white cardstock in half. It should be big enough to display your print. Use glue or tape to stick your print to the front of the card.

PRESSED FLOWER PICTURE

Pressing flowers is a way to **preserve** colorful blossoms. But you have to be patient! It takes a few weeks from the time you cut your flowers for them to be ready.

MATERIALS

- Scissors
- Various types of flowers
- Lots of large, heavy books, all about the same size
- Two pieces of thin cardboard (like the front and back of a cereal box)
- Two sheets of white copy paper
- Tweezers
- Cardstock paper
- A picture frame
- White glue

STEPS

1. Take a nature walk. Snip fresh flowers that you love. Try not to cut any blooms when they are wet. Look for blossoms that can lie flat. They shouldn't have thick centers. They shouldn't have too many layers of petals.

2. Place a book onto your workspace. Cut both pieces of cardboard and paper. They should be about the same size as the cover of the book. Then place one piece of cardboard and one piece of white paper onto the book.

If a flower is too thick, remove some petals.

3. Trim the stems off the flowers. Place the flowers facedown on the white paper. Lay them as flat as possible. If a flower is too thick, you can pluck some of the petals from the center. Make sure none of the flowers overlap on the paper.

4. Place the other piece of white paper on top of the flowers. Put the other piece of cardboard on top of the paper. Gently place another heavy book on top of the cardboard.

5. Place all of the other heavy books on the stack. Make sure you have set up your flower-press tower in a place where it won't get in anyone's way.

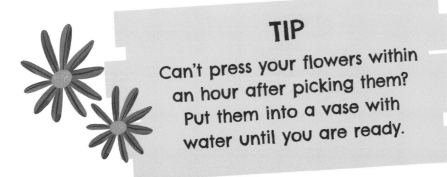

TIP

Can't press your flowers within an hour after picking them? Put them into a vase with water until you are ready.

6. After about two or three weeks, carefully remove the books. See your pressed flowers. They will be very delicate. Carefully take them off the paper. Use tweezers if needed.

7. Cut the cardstock to the same size as your picture frame. Use tweezers to arrange the flowers on it. When you are happy, dab white glue on a few points around the back of each flower. Set them back in place gently.

8. Let the glue dry completely. Put the frame's glass over the picture. Put it in the frame.

SAND CANDLES

Can you dig it? Dig in the sand! You can use the shapes you make as molds for candles. Do you live at the beach? You can make these candles right on the sand. Just make sure you put up a sign. You don't want anyone to disturb them while they cool. Ask an adult to help you with this project.

MATERIALS

- Large plastic bucket or bowl
- Sand
- Spray bottle filled with water
- Two old pots no longer used for cooking, one large and one small
- Old or broken candles
- Wooden skewers
- Prepared wicks for votive candles (from the craft store)
- Scissors

STEPS

1. Fill the bucket with sand. Make it about 4 to 5 inches (10 to 12.7 cm) deep. Test to see if your sand is moist enough. Squeeze some in your hand. It should clump. If it is too dry, spray it with water until it clumps.

SEE NEXT PAGE

2. Dig out a space in the sand about 2 to 3 inches (5 to 7.6 cm) deep. You can dig out any shape you want. Make sure the bottom of your hole is flat. That way the candle will sit level when it is done.

3. Fill the large pot with about 3 inches (7.6 cm) of water. Place it on the stove. Heat the water until it boils. Turn down the heat to simmer. Place the smaller pot into the larger pot. Add the old candles to the smaller pot. Heat them until they are fully melted. Stir with the skewers.

SAFETY TIPS

Do not heat the pot with the candles directly over the heat source. Do not heat the wax to more than 180 degrees Fahrenheit (82 degrees Celsius). Use a craft or candy thermometer to check the temperature. Wax is very flammable. Never leave it unattended while heating.

4. Pour the melted wax into the molds. Pour until it is level with the top of the sand. Place a wick into each candle. If some of the wax is absorbed into the sand, fill the molds back to the top.

5. Let the candles cool completely. This may take a few hours. Gently remove them when they are cool. Brush off the extra sand.

6. Before you light your candle, trim the wick to 0.25 inches (0.6 cm). Place it on a candle tray or plate.

CRITTER-FRIENDLY CORNER

Nature has provided you with so many materials. Now it's time to give back. Give back to the creatures that live there! Here are some ideas to make an animal-friendly corner in a yard or garden.

- Gather rocks to make a stone wall. Chipmunks use stone walls for quick getaways.

- Place a broken ceramic pot upside down. Make a toad house.

- Make a birdbath from a ceramic or plastic pot saucer. Place it on a pile of flat stones. It should be about 12 inches (30 cm) high. Weigh down the center with another stone. Fill it with water.

- Make a bird feeder out of a plastic tray. Weigh down the center with a rock. Fill in the area around the rock with birdseed.

INSPIRATION EVERY DAY

Bring nature into your life. Glance out the window. Take a walk. By making a nature craft, you can interact with all of the inspiration and resources of the outdoors. Once you start making nature crafts, plants won't be the only things growing: your new ideas will, too!

A good way to keep track of your ideas is with a nature sketchbook. Keep a small notepad and a pencil in your pocket. Draw pictures of leaves, flowers, or other natural items you see. Can't go outside? You can flip through your sketchbook and be inspired by nature!

GLOSSARY

blot (BLAHT) to dry by soaking up excess liquid

burrow (BUHR-oh) a tunnel or hole in the ground made or used as a home by an animal

endangered (in-DAYN-juhrd) at risk of dying out

minerals (MIH-nuh-ruhls) solid substances found in Earth that do not come from plants or animals

palette (PAH-luht) a flat surface for holding or mixing paint

preserve (prih-ZERV) to protect something so that it stays in its original state

sachet (sah-SHAY) a small bag filled with items that give off a pleasant smell

tendrils (TEHN-druhls) threadlike, curly plant parts

textures (TEKS-churz) the different ways things feel, such as how rough or smooth they are

FOR MORE INFORMATION

BOOKS

Doudna, Kelly. *Super Simple Pinecone Projects*: *Fun and Easy Crafts Inspired by Nature*. Minneapolis: ABDO Publishing Company, 2014.

Martin, Laura C. *Nature's Art Box*. North Adams, MA: Storey Kids, 2003.

Rhatigan, Joe. *The Kids' Guide to Nature Adventures*. New York: Lark Books, 2003.

Tornio, Stacy, and Ken Keffer. *Kids' Outdoor Adventure Book*. Guilford, CT: Falcon Guides, 2013.

INDEX

animals, 9, 28

biomes, 5

candles project, 25–27
clay, 6
colors, 5
conservation, 9
critter-friendly corner project, 28

fabrics, 7
fibers, 7
flower picture project, 22–24
fossil stepping-stone project, 16–17

grapevine wreath project, 12–13

hammered leaf prints project, 20–21

indoor supplies, 10
inspiration sources, 4–5, 29

leaf prints project, 20–21

minerals, 6

nature
    observation and appreciation,
    4–5, 29

resources, 6–7, 8–9

observing nature, 4–5, 29
outdoor supplies, 8–9

painting tips, 10
pine sachet project, 14–15
pressed flower picture project, 22–24
projects, 12–28

sand candles project, 25–27
sewing tips, 11
shell wind chimes project, 18–19
sketchbooks, 29
stepping-stone project, 16–17
stitching, 11
supplies, 8–11, 10, 12, 16, 18, 20,
    22, 25
sustainable collecting, 9

textiles, 7
textures, 5

wind chimes project, 18–19